Hey World,
I'm Unleashed!

The Heart & Soul
of an Inspired Dreamer...

By:
Cassandra Lennox

Write World
Press

Printed in the United States of America
Write World Press
ISBN 978-1-7328017-5-2

For information on permissions, freelance writing, or other services, please write to:
contact@cassandralennox.com
www.cassandralennox.com

To Lil...
My precious first born.

I began writing this
when you came into my life...
and taught me that dreams
truly do come true.

It is the greatest honor,
To impact others' lives.

That is how, my friends,
We <u>truly</u> soar.

Thank you-

To all who have held my hand and believed in me on this crazy ride. Your uplifting encouragement, the strength you provided in moments of weakness, your words of wisdom and the value you have brought to my life is immeasurable. I admire, respect, and am eternally grateful to you all.

To those who have led me to tears, I forgive and I truly appreciate you. It's part of the human experience and the words that came from those less than stellar times are beautiful and profound. I hope you have learned and grown from it all, as have I. Onward and upward. I hope you are happy and living honest and true.

To those I've met in passing, there is always a reason for the encounter. I'm glad for each hello, each brief moment of time, even if I'll never see you again. Something as small as a smile or a laugh may have sparked a poem, or turned my day around, or yours. Oftentimes, it is truly about the little things in life.

To those no longer with us who have made a significant impact in my life. I know you are watching over us and you know that the impact you made in your time here is recognized and appreciated every single day. I am so proud to have guardian angels shining down on us. You are forever in my mind and heart.

To those I haven't met yet, perhaps my words will spark something in you. Perhaps you'll relate. Hopefully you'll find inspiration somewhere along the lines and you'll in turn inspire another, or many, and create a chain of inspiration.

Thank you <u>all</u>. I appreciate the guidance, grace, lessons, and love.

I'm no longer feeling trapped, begging the world to realize that "I am someone, too!"

It is because of you, because of that past, because of this present… and the beautiful hope, trust, and belief that I have grown to have in myself and the future…

*That I am **unleashed**!*

Thank you all… from the depths of my crazy beautiful, over-emotional, poetic and determined heart.

I love you. I am grateful, and I ask you please, unleash yourself to the world…

Contents

Preface-

My thoughts to you… (Late December 2020)

This was initially meant to be "calmer." This book was originally intended to be released in simpler, normal times, whatever that means. Pre-pandemic, basically. The way I saw the world when that ball dropped to ring in 2020.

This book was 10 years in the making. After publishing "Hey World, I'm Someone Too!" in 2010, I knew that was just the beginning of allowing my words out into the world and that there would be a follow up book someday.

I, of course, did not know that 2020 would be what it is. It became a revelation of truth and reality.

What do we value? What do we strive for? What truly matters?

What do we love and what can we let go of?

It requires a deep breath… for moments… or months.

What will change and what will be?

The uncertainty is real. But I know there is no good to come out of hesitation in being real and releasing.

So here it is. From me to you. No holds barred.

It's quite different than "Hey World, I'm Someone Too!"

That was younger me, in my teenage years. I was Cassie Villano.

Now I use my full name. I'm married and have four beautiful children, but that is only a portion of how I have changed and grown. Much of this book is from the past 10 years, some is just this past year.

It's all real. It's all raw. It's how I've processed what I've learned from others and wrote the words to express it. It's taking the experiences and putting it on paper and releasing my emotions in the best way I know how.

I have had quite a roller-coaster adventure (cliché, but I don't care. The analogy is real. Maybe It's why I love roller coasters.)

Some of the words in this book have been inspired by the remarkable people in my life, who I am so blessed to have and know.

They share a story, I strive to understand and interpret it best I can, I put it to words, and we find and enhance that human connection.

Much of this book is the inner workings of my imaginative mind and increasing determination as I experience life, even from beautifully broken angles.

This is my "Hey, I'm letting this out now, because it's time to do so. My heart, the universe, intuition, whatever you want to call it, feels that I need to get this book out… Now."

If it resonates with someone, my heart will soar. I have always dreamed of positively impacting others, but I was shy, scared, reserved, because I was afraid of what people would think when I let the words out.

If you don't resonate, that's fine. No one in the world can please or resonate with everyone. No hard feelings.

If you do resonate, here's a hug from me to you. I'll smile at the world right at your side, from the beautifully broken angles, the peak of the mountain, or the first rung of the ladder climbing out of the rut, it doesn't matter. What matters is that you start somewhere.

And my friend, please note, the world may not always understand you, and I know they don't always understand me.

That's more than ok.

There's a unique and beautiful glisten, a sparkle that *only you* can exude.

Embrace it…

Trust it…

And _Unleash._

I'm Unleashed!" -

Once upon a time,
a dreaming teenage girl,
Knew with all her heart
she had a message for the world.

After years of hesitation,
she knew what she had to do,
So she compiled it all together,
as "Hey World, I'm Someone Too!"

It was a message she needed to let out,
after years of being so unsure.
She gathered up the courage,
took a deep breath as she reached for more.

It was scary, there's no doubt,
she didn't know what she was doing,
But deep within her mind,
a creative storm was brewing.

So she finally published the book,
and let the words run free,
She always knew deep within,
this is what was meant to be.

And over years those words she shared
made people cry and smile,
She began to trust this was her purpose
and has been so all awhile.

So continue to write, that she did,
through every up and down.

Moments of stillness and silence,
And the times that were profound.

For she knew that was the thing about life,
the valleys and peaks we endure,
There's purpose beneath the layers
that is real and strong and pure.

She dreamed of making an impact,
inspiring those all around,
Picking up all the pieces of doubt
that were scattered across the ground.

It was time to make herself whole again,
it was time to stand up and fight.
There's a fire within her soul
That was just waiting to ignite.

But it was she who needed to fuel it,
to bring the spark aglow,
To inspire and encourage,
to release, persist and grow.

There was something to declare,
and it was time, she vowed.
"Hey World, I'm Unleashed!"
She spoke the words aloud.

And as she heard her voice speak out,
It all became so clear,
This is where the next book begins,
Right now and right here…

In this Moment -

Close your eyes,
Get a glimpse of what your life can be.
Settle your thoughts,
Open your mind and set yourself free.

There is a story unfolding,
The legacy of you,
A breath of the words
of your dreams coming true.

Just listen.
The answers are there.
Take a moment to pause.
Inhale the truth in the air.

Moments are priceless,
Be wise how you spend.
Each second is a blessing
Just as each lesson, a friend.

Allow your heart to uncover,
Your truth and your voice,
To hide or be seen,
You are blessed with the choice.

Make that decision,
Then open your eyes,
And begin that climb
To soaring the skies…

"The girl was beautifully broken, hiding behind a smile. Now she's picking up the pieces that have been there all awhile."

It was not an alarm clock
That finally awakened me.
It was my own voice.
My own thoughts.
My own heart-
Telling me it was time to wake the hell up
And live my life.

Revelation -

For years I've been walked on, criticized and torn down,
And the time has come to turn that all around.

I reflect on my weaknesses and assure myself it's ok.
Tell myself strength is something that grows day by day.

This belief in myself, it took time to build,
To develop a confidence, to be bold and strong-willed.

I'm no longer that girl, who bowed down to the lies,
The past is the past and I've said all my goodbyes.

I guess some do not realize how strong I have become,
They can see me as timid, or weak, or even dumb.

But what matters is that I know, who I am and will be,
My eyes are now wide open, and I can clearly see.

And when I look in the mirror, a smile looks right back.
With self-love much more powerful than anything I lack.

I assure myself, I trust it, I know the time is now.
To take back my control, right here I make that vow.

*"Let what's within you ignite the spark,
so you can be that which lights up the dark."*

The 5 Minute Poem -

Five little minutes,
Can I create a rhyme?
That holds meaning and reason,
In that bit of time?

What is there to say?
Do I discuss my day?
I am Me, so I will find a way.

I'm going to write about what's on my mind.
About all I have found and what I will find.

Today has been magical to say but the least.
My mindset spot on, my optimism increased.

I feel really great, about that I can't lie.
I feel like my life is a force I cannot deny.

I feel powerful, manifesting, real and true.
I feel like the pages are finding their due.

The words are rewritten, my life was a draft,
I'll spend the rest of my years perfecting my craft.

And what helps the world, my legacy will be.
And the rest of it is what helps me be me.

I'm selfish at times, the rest I give all.
I no longer frown when I cry, or I fall.

I'm glad to be real, I'm glad that I feel.
To God and the world, I'm happy to kneel.

I'm blessed with these gifts, and even the curse,
So many people in this world have worse.

To me it's ok, I'll be what I be.
You please be you, the world will see.

Writing Poetry-

My refuge.
Release,
Revelation.

Where I create my own rules,
Design my own beginning.
My own end.

The middle bleeds truth in its purest form.
It trickles down,
Like tears.

The words dance across the page,
Blurring together,
Blissfully aware that they have found their place.

I'm just a girl with a pen
And a blank piece of paper.

Capturing each moment.
Creating her life.

When negativity swirls around you,
Like you are the eye
Of the storm.

Wind blows fiercely
Intimidating
And you cannot catch your breath.

Remember the previous moment,
The calm before the storm.
The peace.
Serenity.

The clouds will part.
The sun will shine again.

Trust.
Know.
You will survive.
You will thrive.

It's Ok to be Vulnerable -

Vulnerability.

I once thought it to be a weakness... a fault...negative.

Even the thesaurus gives this word a bad name. "Susceptible, weak, defenseless."

But then there's one synonym... "Openness."

Well now, that's a game changer.

I don't want to be susceptible, weak, or defenseless.

Yet "open"... I'll be open, because it is worthwhile. There is much in life to be open to.

But... what if I'm *susceptible* to support and help to achieve goals and dreams... what if I recognize my *weaknesses* so that I can learn and increase my strength, what if I need to be *defenseless* for just a moment while I build that strong foundation on which the walls will protect, the tower will be built, that foundation on which to grow and flourish, and make an impact...

Maybe being vulnerable isn't a bad thing.

Maybe it's Step One.

Maybe it's laying the groundwork. It's the canvas for our tapestry. The blank page on which we write our story. The premise on which we build our business. Or the landing on which we jump from that throws us onto the path we were meant to be, on which we will thrive throughout our lives...

Don't knock vulnerability. Don't look down on it, don't give it a bad name.

Sometimes people are vulnerable because they need a change, a friend, a realization. Maybe they are vulnerable because they are ready to take a stand and truly LIVE.

We need to start somewhere. And even when we are far in, when we are doing great things, there are moments of vulnerability. Where we are willing to be susceptible, or weak, or appear defenseless, because we are REAL. We are Human. We all have "moments." It's how we react to those moments... how we take the next step after the moment has passed.

That is what matters.

I'll be vulnerable at times. And I won't pass judgement when you do, either. I'll take your hand. And tell you it's ok. Let's be "vulnerable" together.

Let's live out our purpose...

*"The voice in our head is not the enemy.
It is there to motivate us to prove it wrong."*

Grateful -

I am grateful for the reflection that I see,
The sparkle in my eyes as I declare, yes, that's me.

I am grateful for the moments that have made me strong,
For the times that it felt everything went wrong.

I'm grateful for the things I used to overlook,
A warm cup of coffee, my current book.

My children's laughter, even at 6 in the morn,
How a new chapter began as each was born.

I'm grateful for the little things,
Rhyme and poetry and the joy it brings.

Sparkle and humor and a glass of wine.
The quirky qualities that I call mine.

For yesterday's story and tomorrows song,
I'm writing today, as I've been all along.

Grateful for so much, I'll recognize each day,
That gratitude can go such a very long way.

In changing and growing when push comes to shove,
I'm grateful to be living a life that I love.

*"Opening your mind, will open a door.
While opening your heart will give you more."*

Dreamers & Doers -

I spent so many years caught up in dreaming,
Just dreaming of a perfect world,
Where things played out as planned,
Where it spun in sync with how I twirled.

I wished on stars and skipping rocks,
I prayed before I slept.
I found the rainbow's colors,
after the tears that I had wept.

I did everything I was supposed to,
or at least at the time I thought,
I followed most of the rules,
And I did what I was taught.

So why wasn't my life playing out,
like younger me had dreamed?
If I gave it my true all,
could I still be redeemed?

I accept my imperfections,
but still I've tried my best,
Why did life just throw me curveballs,
a constant, tiring test?

Maybe it was telling me,
"Hey, there are more than dreams.
Life can be so beautiful,
but it's not what it seems."

Dreams achieved don't mean perfection,
nor is happiness a destination,
This was my total turning point,
this was my revelation.

It's not about the dreaming, friends,
it's about the dream that lives,
It's about not what a person takes,
but about what a person gives.

Maybe you, too, spent years dreaming,
And wishing on a star,
You know you are meant for grander things,
You believe you can go so far.

There is a time for each of us,
And perhaps yours is here and now,
It's time to make a promise,
A true and solemn vow.

A promise to yourself,
You'll make the dreams take flight.
You will do what it takes, release the brakes.
And uncover your brightest light.

And when you pause in doubt,
Just remember who you truly are,
The dreamer who is a do-er
Who once wished upon a star.

And you, like I, will scale mountains,
We will reach to the greatest peak.
There is power in numbers,
A supported heart will not be weak.

There is such beauty in the journey,
Despite the highs and lows,
It's not a matter of going,
Only which way the wind then blows.

We go the direction our heart leads us,
With our friends an arm's reach away,
We will be everything we've ever dreamed,
Forever and a day.

"Sometimes we must venture straight into the storm trusting the sun will protect us and keep us warm."

Road Rage -

On the crazy road of life,
there will be detours along the way.
Sometimes you'll hit a roadblock
and at a standstill you will stay.

But you can use that time wisely,
you don't have to mope and yell.
You're stuck in traffic for goodness sakes,
don't act like you're stuck in hell.

Some people will have road rage
and some won't know where they're going.
Some will act completely reckless
even when rain or snow are blowing.

There will be bridges and mountains
and tunnels through which you'll go.
At times the pace may seem way too fast,
other times much too slow.

Only you can keep your cool,
it's a decision that you make.
You're the one who gets to choose
whether to hit the gas or brake.

So shut your ego into the trunk
and change that vibe right now.
We're on this trip together,
gotta make it through somehow.

Just take the traffic as it comes,
and please do not complain.
Enjoy each mile of the journey
and stay in your own damn lane!

*"When the mind's full of mayhem
and there's chaos, embrace it.
This day only comes once
and you can never replace it."*

Your Message in a Bottle, It's Time to Set it Free -

If you could write just one paragraph…and put your message in a bottle, what would it say?

A question like this one can make us realize how much we have to say. Narrowing it down isn't an easy thing, especially unknowing of your audience.

I had to pause a moment to think. If I have no idea who would be the one to receive my message, what would I want to say, no matter who the recipient is? Most often we are focusing on narrowing down our audience, focusing on our who needs our message the most. So, this is the complete opposite. This is broadening the horizons, just for the sake of taking a moment to see it all from a different perspective.

Therefore, what to say?

I'd say, *"I believe in you."*

The recipient would probably look around the beach, confused, and think "Who? Me?"

"Yes, you! I believe in YOU. I believe you are capable of bringing good to the world. That you have talents beyond your wildest dreams. That you are capable. You are worthy. You possess beauty even if or when you don't see it. You are meant to do great things. You can overcome obstacles and adversity. You can conquer your demons. You can make an impact. You can create a legacy. You can sparkle like the stars, make ripples like waves, and shine like the sun.

You found this message for a reason.

The winds and tides of life brought you here, and this message here, at this moment in time.

Now take your own message. Send it in a bottle. Put it out there in the world"

Share your words with the world because you just never know what your message can do or how far it will go…

Hit Your Head -

There are days we may feel out of line,
A couple paces short of "fine."

When down seems up and up is down,
Some days the answers can't be found.

Sometimes you just want to GO
And things just seem to move so slow.

Some days you just don't feel like you,
It takes all you've got, just to push through.

When you lose your balance or hit your head
And wish you'd stayed in bed instead.

Or you fall down flat upon your face,
Slow down my friend, it's not a race.

Go ahead a moment, pout and cry,
Then wipe and wave those tears goodbye.

Today could be a total pain,
But I bet there's something there to gain.

The lesson that you learn today,
Can help tomorrow in a different way.

And if you fall a few steps back.
It's ok to cut yourself some slack,

Just stay persistent and follow your call,
Remember you are human, after all.

Lean on a loved one or a friend,
Remember, dips propel you up again.

Who cares if one day is the pits,
It's no reason to call it quits,

Tomorrow can be the greatest day,
But friend, that is for you to say.

"Let your tears be the rain that washes doubts away, and your smile be the sun that starts a new day."

What If -

There's a bit beyond believing the things that we can see.
A breath beyond believing in the things that we can be.

A step beyond the know-how, the things now in our hold,
A step beyond the moment, a blissful gleam of gold.

What if you are that person who is meant for so much more,
What if you are that power that can open a sealed door?

What if you are the lyric that is added to the song,
Or the painting of the picture, what if this is where you do
belong?

If you are the answer to what others strive to know,
The light that ignites and sets off a stunning glow.

What if there's no "if," what if there's only what is real,
What if you are everything that your mind and heart both feel?

What if there are no limitations, if you are everything you're
meant,
What if all the past pain and failure, are time so very well
spent?

Maybe there is reason, maybe there is rhyme,
Maybe we didn't realize that we knew it all this time.

We are all meant for something, that is greater than just a
dream,
Success and truth and purpose, a life that has a theme.

Tomorrow is not promised, we only make a promise to our
own,

To show the world we have learned, we've thrived, and we have grown.

It's all about the moment, the message and the lesson, too. The light in utter darkness, the voice that speaks so true.

"Stepping out of your comfort zone is stepping into a world of beauty unknown."

Being Over-Emotional. My Biggest Fault and Greatest Quality -

So many of us, myself included, talk about how life is a journey, a roller coaster, and an adventure.

All of this is true.

But I don't know if that really encompasses the height and depth that so many of us feel, sometimes alternating, even in a single day.

Growing up, I was told I'm too emotional. Back then, sometimes hearing that would make me cry.

Flash forward a few years … after hitting rock bottom… after grasping the past, after boarding one of life's craziest roller coasters, after soaring the skies… I changed my perspective on that a bit.

I say this metaphorically, but literally as well. I hit rock bottom and discovered that beer and fast food only numbs the pain but doesn't get us past it (before I became a mom) … I grasped a lifeboat davit (#13) recovered from the wreck of the Titanic… I rode the most badass roller coaster in Tokyo, Japan after a 2.5 hour wait because some of the greatest thrills in life are truly worth the wait… and I soared the skies not just in airplanes but with a parachute, above the sparking blue waters of Hawaii.

I could go on… but I digress.

Life itself is more intense than some people realize. When they look at another, especially when they judge another, it's crucial to understand that even if we cannot see the world through their eyes, they can and do. Our experiences are uniquely ours and therefore our stories are as well.

Our passions, our truths, skills, dreams, purpose and drive… sometimes even that feels like it changes especially during rougher times. But does it really? Or is it the constant?

Some people will relate to you, some will not.

Some will judge. Some will talk.

Others will appreciate and be inspired.

A long time ago, I came to terms with being what some may call "very emotional," or something of that sort.

I don't recall the day my reaction to that changed, but I know I've heard it said numerous times over the years.

I don't get upset about it. Instead I smile, agree, and respond, "I know. It's my biggest fault, and my greatest quality."

If I didn't take experiences to heart, the words wouldn't flow as they do.

I let it out through writing. Whether it's the peak of the roller coaster or the deepest of the dips. Whether it's the thrill of the freefall downfall or the terror of being pushed out of the airplane.

Life is more than a journey.

It's a greater ride than any roller coaster ever could be.

And an adventure… yes… our own unique adventure that we have the power to create.

I'm glad I'm "so emotional."

It makes me… me.

And I don't care to be anyone different.

The stories I'll someday tell will relate to the people who are told they "feel too deeply… or dream too big… or believe too much."

So anymore… people want to tell me I'm too emotional?

In return they'll likely get a high five, a thank you, maybe even a hug.

Or an off the cuff poem recited to them, who knows?

All in all…

Be you. Be true.

Own the adventure.

Writing Your Story -

Grab your tissues and your pen,
It's time to visit the past, my friend.

That crazy journey of up and down,
At times it may have spun around.

You picked up some bricks along the way,
But those heavy things don't have to stay.

Process and release your bricks,
You heart will mend and it will fix.

Tears may fall and that's ok,
Keep on writing anyway!

Only you can write this true,
It is a story uniquely you!

So make sure you're honest when you write,
And it will help you see the light,

That there were lessons that you learned,
Even when you crashed and burned.

It's hard to drop the bricks you own,
But remember, friend, you're not alone!

You'll feel much stronger once they're gone,
And we are here to cheer you on!

"You can change your story, for you hold the pen.

If this chapter isn't working, then write it again."

Living my Best Life Now -

I've always dreamed of being better,
yet I thought I didn't know how.
Then I began to learn
about living my best life now.

I've learned all the things "I Am",
and to believe it in every way.
That self-care is crucial
and to engage in it each day.

I learned to have a positive mindset,
and pay attention to every thought,
To use my vision board to inspire me,
and remind me if I forgot.

Use my words of the year to guide me,
grow and sparkle all year through.
To keep a good attitude
despite what others say or do.

That stress is not always bad
and can often be reduced,
Sometimes the smallest changes
can give you quite a boost.

How to make decisions,
allowing emotions to play their parts.
To prevent anxiety,
and handle it whenever it starts.

Negative self-talk is sabotage,
and it comes in many forms,
Self-awareness, however,
can help us defy the norms.

When it comes to success and happiness,
confidence is key.
And all these put together
reveal who we are meant to be.

I've learned that I'm so much more than a writer,
a mother and a wife.
I'm sparkling and growing,
and I'm learning to live my best life!

"First and foremost believe in YOU.

It's the ultimate key to your dreams coming true."

For the Woman Who Will Take on the World -

I am more than the mirror reflects me to be.
There is fire behind these eyes,
it burns wild, courageous, free.

I am louder than the voices inside of my head.
They speak negativity,
but I speak truth and faith instead.

I am stronger than the tears that sometimes fall,
When the rain dries again,
I stand proud and tall.

I am braver than the hesitation I feel,
When push comes to shove,
I know what is real.

I am greater than the failures in my past,
The pain subsides,
And I embrace the lessons at last.

I am capable more than some may think.
And I won't dim my light,
Or bow down or shrink.

Growing, in my sincerest and greatest form,
I am here to take the world by storm.

You can be still -
You can be a gust of wind -
Or you can take the world by storm.

Their Legacy Lives On –

There are faces we see so clearly,
Though only in our mind,
Within treasured photographs,
& in our dreams from time to time.

We often feel a void inside,
Despite the memories all along.
Their voice whispers to us in the wind,
Just as the rain will sing their song.

The bonds can remain strong forever,
Even when those we love pass on.
They remain within our hearts
And their impact is never gone.

We look at what their time has taught us,
And the memories we embrace,
Recalling the sparkle in their eye,
The smile upon their face.

We remember the stories those eyes told,
That journey that makes us so proud,
We're reminded of them daily,
As the sunlight streams through the clouds.

That sparkle is for always,
And that smile will always be.

The words they spoke and love they gave,
Will forever live on free.

Their legacy everlasting,
From all they did and gave,
There's a ripple they created,
And it's up to us to catch the wave.

Would You Climb 100 Flights of Stairs if it Meant Reaching Your Goals?

An enormous staircase loomed before me. It went up so high, I couldn't see what was beyond the many stairs.

A voice said to me, "Will you climb 100 flights of stairs if it means reaching your goals?"

Without hesitation, "Absolutely," I replied.

Then I awoke.

I laid in bed for a few minutes, realizing just how metaphorical the dream was.

In life, we are all presented with a "staircase." (Or a series, thereof!)

We choose to take that first step. We choose our pace. When we find ourselves at a standstill, we aren't falling back down, we are simply at a landing in between flights. When we do take our next step, we are moving forward and upward.

Even though it was a dream, I wasn't lucid. I didn't realize I was dreaming so course I saw this staircase as real. My immediate response of "absolutely," fills me with pride. There was no hesitation, no doubt, no excuses. Just a full-on commitment to tackle all 100 flights of stairs to reach those goals.

Our "staircases" are not always evenly spaced. They may slant, become steep, and even be without a railing to hold onto. Despite the condition of the individual stairs, they are still providing a solid space to step on the uphill venture.

I'm reminded of Koko Head in Hawaii. Years ago, a friend and I climbed to the top. The climb was not easy for me. The condition of the "stairs" was terrifying. The wood was rotted, it was very steep in areas, there were huge gaps, and the fall would not have been pretty to say the least.

I was so worried of a misstep and falling. I'm sometimes clumsy. It's related to hearing impairment, but that's a story for another time.

It took quite a while. I wasn't in the greatest physical shape of my life and hadn't been on a hike of any sort in a long time. But somehow or other, I stayed focused and determined and made it to top of the Koko Head Crater Trail. The 1,000 or so stairs were well worth it. The view was breathtaking, but just as beautiful was that feeling of accomplishment, of pushing on when things got hard.

Would I do it again? Absolutely!

Tackle your staircase. Take that first step. You'll reach something amazing, and the journey along the way is bound to be incredible.

Remember that the adventure can often be as beautiful as the destination.

Beautiful You -

You beautiful soul, who hides in the shadows,
Is that a tear falling down your cheek?
Is it guidance you seek?
Is it a voice to tell you to emerge from that space?
Let yourself be seen?
Are you fearful of the words you really do mean?

The shadows don't flatter you, your light must shine bright,
Take one step at a time, into the light.
There are arms wide open, to welcome you.
To allow your beauty and truth to shine through.

You beautiful mind, who hides in the shadows,
Is that chaos spinning through your head?
Is it guidance you crave instead?
Is it a shoulder to lean on as you emerge from that space?
Let yourself be real?
Are you hesitant of the words you really do feel?

The shadows don't flatter you, your truth must be told,
Take one step at a time, find your gold.
There are arms wide open, to embrace you tight.
To allow your beauty and truth to ignite.

"The greatest and brightest lights are not cast by those who have it all, but by those who encounter the darkness and find the smallest embers from which they create their fire."

I See You -

I see you –
Beyond the external, behind the smile.

I see you –
Through adversity and every trial.

Far beyond, behind and below,
Your dreams and hopes, the depths of your soul.

I see the light that shines in the dark,
In the bleakest night, it ignites a spark.

I see the dreamer, the creator, the rhyme.
A legacy in the making to stand the test of time.

A story to be told, the pages await.
Why settle for good when you know you'll be great?

I see you –
Pure. Honest and true.

But what matters most, is that YOU see YOU.

*"With each small victory you grasp a star.
Gather enough stars and you can illuminate the world."*

The Power to Shine -

We can look back at the past, with a laugh, a smile a tear.

At the beautiful and broken road that has led to now and here.

A means to fill our purpose, to truly live, and feel alive.

An impact on the world, it is for that which we all strive.

Our story, our message, or poem or work of art,

Finding that truth within us, from which we may have grown apart.

Our search has been for guidance that illuminates the way,

A candle with a burning wick that tells us it's ok.

We are dreamers, we are doers, we are seekers, and we are light.

Even dimmed by all the years, we have the power to shine so bright.

"Everyone has a light.

It's up to you how brightly <u>yours</u> will shine."

A Dream Now Seen, A Voice Now Heard -

I lived much of my childhood in the shadows.

I was the girl who always fell a few steps short and felt like the sunlight cast a glare that made her invisible to the world…

A creative mind and heart yearning to do and be something real…

A beautiful canvas of unspoken words, picturesque dreams, and lonely poetry.

While my thoughts were deafening to me, others heard silence.

Something inside told me that this was the way it needed to be. That something was a dark, deflating voice of self-doubt, imperfection and pity.

The voice produced some exquisite poems and stories at the time. It scribbled across endless pages of notebooks, journals, post its, and chalkboards.

It cried into the night and I cried along with it.

Then one day, I did the unthinkable…

I shared my words.

Hesitant and fearful, I began to let the world in… allow the sun's rays to hit me… I took that one little step out of the shadows and into the sunlight. I let just one poem out into the world… into "This World." That was the title.

Until this moment of journaling for this prompt, I hadn't realized the significance of that one being the first poem I wrote with the actual intention of sharing it.

I recall reading it aloud to my friend. I saw the beam in her eye. I'll never forget the smile on her face.

I felt *seen* for the first time. My words were appreciated, and not just by my pens and notebooks.

I remember thinking, "Maybe these words *aren't* just for me."

Maybe we choose our visibility by our openness, vulnerability, willingness to BE SEEN.

I think the actual interpretation of the feelings and the words were slightly different then. I was 14 years old at the time.

23 years later, I look back at the process of dissipating the shadows and unraveling the lies I told myself.

It was a long sequence of baby steps. Releasing my words into the world. Letting some resonate with others. Some were less than received. It was an up and down journey.

I've always loved rollercoasters. The up and down, that's not a metaphor. That's just life.

When you go down fast, it can propel you back up…

There are moments in life, that you just know you have to release.

Whether it's your words, your feelings, your goals, or your truth.

We are here for a limited time. Cast away the shadows while you can.

I had to realize this very gradually, and I accept that.

There were accumulating moments when I could assure myself that I was no longer the invisible being, scared of the world, fearful of being herself.

Being visible doesn't always mean being visible to everyone. It is being visible to SOMEONE, in that moment.

Making an impact. Doing good. Being appreciated. Fulfilling a purpose.

It's not always about the scope of your visibility. It's the authenticity behind it.

If someone sees you… or creates a memory in that moment with you, or is touched by your words, or your voice, or your art, or your mission…

When you do something that helps a person from one moment to the next, you are *seen*.

You are no longer a gust of wind, a wishful thought, a still silence.

You are visible. You are beautiful. You are meant.

And whatever you do, please, never allow anyone to hold you down within the shadows.

Remember that your light can shine from any angle.

Here is the "This World" poem, written back in the 8th grade. The poems I put out there to the world have evolved since then, but these are the words of a 14-year girl who was realizing how much she wanted to inspire and help others, to be seen so that she could help others be seen.

This World –

"Stare at the past,
it's a treasured story
that lit the road for today.

Dream of the present,
it's a continuing battle,
a battle that won't fade away.

Look toward tomorrow,
it's a hidden dream,
that will soon bring forth to the light.

Learn the meaning of life,
all that we face,
the endless struggle and fight.

Hold the heart of a friend,
a precious smile
a bond that will never die.

Keep faith in a love
who will hold you dear
and never say good-bye.

Shine through your tears,
it's not worth the pain,
to regret what's already been.

Make the most of each day,
it only comes once,
and will never be seen again.

Life is a challenge,
a test we must take,
a journey through bad and good.

This world's a mystery,
still left unsolved,
that may someday be understood.

Continue to hope,
a miracle may happen
to make all dreams come true.

Strive for the best,
let your laughter be heard
to make up for what you can't undo.

Don't give up,
and don't give in.
Believe in yourself instead.

Open your heart,
overcome your fears,
and you can face what lies ahead."

If I could bottle up my yesterdays would I cast them into the ocean to be carried away?

No, I would keep most of them upon my shelf, for they are what made me who I am today.

You stare into the eyes of your friend.-
And she stares back.
You both smile.
You both cry.
You both laugh.
Your dreams align.
And if there is a moment
That you cannot see her clearly,
Wipe the smudge off the mirror.
And make eye contact again...

I AM -

I am Strength when adversity comes my way.

I am Gratitude for the blessings in my life each day.

I am Attitude when I need to stand up proud and tall.

I am Mindful of my surroundings both big and small.

I am Real in purest form and I do not hide.

I am Determined and hold my hands up for the ride.

I am Honest with others and myself as well.

I am Courageous as I write the tale I'll tell.

I am Success because I continue to grow.

I am Light and I strive to share my glow.

I am High-Vibe and intentionally aligned.

I am Beautiful and know I'm uniquely designed.

I am Confident because I believe in me.

I am Loved.

I am Love.

And that love sets me free.

"Your perception of happy is yours and yours alone."

Let Your Voice be Heard -

It's time to stand tall, you're not that little girl,
Who hides behind closed doors, fearful of the world.

It's time to reach further, to stretch your lengths,
As you develop the power, the tools, and the strengths.

Cut that chain, let it fade away,
It's held you before, but not today.

You come to see that the darkness is not true.
There's a dazzling fire that burns, inside of you.

Don't keep it contained, it can light up the world,
Sparkling, or neon, or shiny, or pearled.

What really matters is that light is your own,
It's brighter than the any of the ties that you've known.

You're stronger than the chains that tug and that pull,
You are a vessel, determination your fuel.

So take a great leap, and blaze a trail,
Frayed ends of a broken rope will just a tell a tale,

Of the path you ventured, of a past left behind,
Now with limitless potential and strong state of mind.

Confidence unearthed from the weight that you held,
You may have failed, but now it's time you excelled.

Declare your independence, let your heart run free,
Step into the life and the beauty you're meant to see.

It's here. It's now. You have the choice.
You're all grown up, now unleash your voice.

"Whoever said you are one in a million was wrong.

You are the one and only you."

Being Me, My Reminder to Self -

What makes me smile and fuels my fire.
Is making words rhyme and using them to inspire,

I can usually find the right words to say,
To relate to others in a special way.

I'm great at seeing the bright side in life,
And finding the lessons in times of strife.

I'm a good listener and I love to learn,
And I view each day as a page we turn.

I transform life experiences into words on the page,
And convey my message with passion when upon a stage.

My greatest joy is being a mom of four,
Teaching them love and persistence, so they too can soar.

I have a way of lifting others up,
And contagious smiles just fill my cup.

There are many things I strive to be,
But what I'm best at is being ME.

The habits...
They break us down,
They pull us under.
One step forward,
Then one back.
The habits keep us in chains.
At a standstill,
Yearning for more.
What change can you make,
That will change your life?
What promise can you make yourself today,
That will improve all of your tomorrows?

*"Life is full of little things.
Find beauty in the little things
and you will find beauty in life."*

The Beauty in the Typo -

We all make typos. Little mistakes, small uh-ohs that we need to go back and fix.

As a writer, I do this often.

Also, as a human, you guessed it, I do this often…

The little mistakes and coulda/woulda/shouldas…

I allowed them to haunt me, like the ghost of a typewriter, with no backspace…no delete button… no way to make things right before moving on.

Then I learned to understand that the so-called errors can be illuminating, they can be the nudge, they can propel the change.

As I looked through extensive folders of my writing, reliving the past 15 years or so, I felt a vast array of emotions.

I wrote, reflecting on the experience,

I typed, "This is a life story…"

But as I re-read it, I saw the typo.

"This is a lift story…"

A *lift* story.

And that's when I realized, it's that, too. Woah.

Not only was I writing about how I lifted myself up after falls and failures, but I realized those experiences will help lift others.-

The passionate, optimistic, determined.

The hurt, the sad, the worn out, the lonely.

The creative, the unsure.

The cursed and the blessed.

I've felt like all of these things at one point.

Recollecting on the past years has shown me this.

Experiencing the present, has justified this notion.

Envisioning the future… Yes. I truly believe, I am ALL of these things.

And it is divine beauty.

I'll take it.

I will bo mo. Dcspitc all sctbacks, faults, unccrtainty and fear.

There are lessons behind the mistakes,

there is a gift with every flaw,

and there is beauty in a typo.

A kaleidoscope of dreams
Every time I see one clearly,
It turns.
Distorting my vision,
Second guessing my path.
So many colors
So many choices.
What to create?
Which dream to grasp on to?

No Regrets -

An internal interrogation
Of past and future situation,

A mindless contemplation
And my own mindset of always reasoning why.

Why some never realize what they have,
Why some will take whatever's up for grabs,

Why people will fill their heart with plenty,
But only speak their mind when they've had too many.

I stood there, danced there, more than a face in the crowd,
Made myself noticed even with the music too loud,

I can still hear the words, that the slurred voices say,
I grin, and I smile, and just turn away.

I'm here, and I'm there, an eternal friend,
I won't change my mind, my stance they can't bend.

And looking around, I hold my head high,
Without second glance, with no regretful sigh.

To me it's perfection, I know what I stand to lose,
Nothing brings me down, when it's what I choose,

They can have regrets, it's part of life in its own,
It's the poetic voice, of each wind that has blown.

Every night has its meaning like every night meets its dawn,
We live and we laugh, we look back and move on.

I'll never stand quiet, when I have something to say,
I speak my mind, it's truths most honest way.

And now I sit here alone, in this tired old room,
My own spinning thoughts, that my mind can assume,

I'm ok and I'm happy, because I'm writing this down,
Just to look upon it tomorrow at the insight I've found.

Some friendships are eternal, some bonds will not break,
Some trials are endless, some truths cannot fake.

There are moments so wonderful, to make up for those less,
Our lives are a journey, not just a test.

There are people that find their way into our heart,
Just as there is a future, just waiting to start.

*"It doesn't matter how many times you fall,
as long as you get up after them all."*

Mid-Night Thoughts -

Crickets chirping, can barely hear my own thoughts,

But isn't this what I love the most?

The eerie silence, the middle of the night,

The quiet I've come to miss, the ghost.

When my thoughts pour out, my emotions don't blur,

It all makes sense though there is still a stir,

Oh how I miss these moments that make me, "me."

When I feel so alive and I feel so free.

The past and present become one in the same,

I live the life born under my name.

The glory and truth that is my life meaning,

The soul and the heart that inside were bleeding.

It is these moments when my life makes sense,

I feel strong against all the past tense.

I am not afraid, I do not have regret,

And my only fears are those I allow or let,

To sink into this heart that's become so strong,

I've dealt with too much to be strung along,

My power is great, my dreams are in line,

You may put me down, but I'm doing just fine.

I can stare at my life and I can smile,

It may not be perfect but it's my style.

I'll get to be where I want, I believe somehow,

I tried back then, but I'm striving now.

I'm getting there, despite what they say,

I take my dreams in stride, I'm doing it my way.

I believe in my future more than they believed in my past,

These visions, these truths, this determination will last.

It wasn't a question of how or when I'd get there someday,

Just that I would persevere until I find a way.

My dreams are in view, and I am not alone,

The times have changed, and I have grown.

"The path we must take is never a straight line."

Twenty Questions -

We spend years searching… only to find…
Answers that don't seem to fit the questions,
Promises that don't hold any actual promise.
Roads that just suddenly divide.
The discontentment from feeling short of content.

But do we ask the right questions to find answers we seek?
And what would we do with it if we really knew it all?
Would we let go of the mystery that drives us through life?
And would we still get back up if we knew we'd fall?

Will promises mean that life's circumstance won't change?
Do we look at the promises as if they are set in stone?
Can we speak only truth as though we breath in gold?
Do we find we can trust those whom we always known?

Would we like to follow a path that's straight and narrow?
Shy away from opportunity when it beckons our name?
Would we give up all of life's choices, just to have none?
Or re-walk the path from which we just came?

Is contentment really something for which we strive?
Should we just settle for being ok or alright?
Or do we need more, like the rush of feeling alive?
What happiness can be found with a "heart vs. mind" fight?

Would I rather be done searching, allow the answers to come
to me?
Can I only believe promises from hearts loyal as can be?
If I follow a path that allows me to choose once in a while,
Will I be more than content? Will I wear a genuine smile?

*"Vulnerability is not a weakness.
It is the first step in building a foundation for growth,
expansion, and the grasping of one's dreams."*

Lyrics at dusk -

Sometimes we look at the distance we have come and gone
We stare at the times that we strived to be strong,
And we wonder, oh we wonder…
Did I leave my old life in the glimpse of an eye,
Did I ever give thought to those tears I cried?
I don't know, I'll never know… I'll never….

Here I stare at the thoughts, spinning and grinning in the
depths of my mind,
Those thoughts that I thought just moments ago, left behind.

They faded away so quickly with no reminiscence,
Though they fought to the death with that begging resistance.

Because I know what I feel,
I thought I once knew what was real,

But maybe I was too young,
perhaps the words hadn't been sung.

A future awaiting, anticipating, the time I would grow up and
see…

There's a beautiful life, a breath beyond what is real,
A pain that hurts, that only time will heal,

A sacred smile, and shining eyes,
And makes you feel, oh time, how it flies…

I thought I knew love once before,
It was a meaningless kiss, and now I know, nothing more.

But a part of my heart, it burned inside,
And I believe that soulful spark in me had died.

I saw my life, I saw the hope all end,
I swore that hollow grin and wound would not mend.

And then I smiled, after I screamed,
And I saw my life play out, as I had dreamed.

I laid breathless on the sand at night,
Staring up at the stars in silent twilight,

Making a wish, and open for more,
As the waves crashed upon an endless shore.

I let those waves carry on, and carry my past,
Like a broom takes away shattered dreams, shattered glass,

And I lay there in silence, the solitude of my mind,
Till the summer breeze carried all the thoughts behind.

It was a beautiful bliss, a worriless start,
A mirrored mirage in the depths of my heart.

A still photograph in black and white,
Shades of gray of may or might.

"You may not realize you are lost,
until it comes time to find yourself."

Happiness is a Choice that Took Me Years to Decide -

I've recently learned a lot about happiness.

What exactly is happiness? As a child and teenager, I thought it was about having everyone like me, being good at everything, having all A's, being pretty, wearing nice clothes, and getting to do what I want.

In hindsight, I was way off.

If that was my perspective, it's no wonder I wasn't "happy."

I had lots of friends, but there were certainly people that didn't like me.

I was very good at some things, but at others, I totally sucked. (Like team sports! Gym class was my worst enemy.)

All A's. Nope, there was a B here and there, and once a C. (*Gasp!* I was mad at myself for years over that. Perfectionist, much?)

Pretty? I was ok. But I felt overlooked. I thought the pretty girls had it made. Comparing myself to them gave me a feeling of inadequacy that lasted for years.

Nice clothes... well I never had much fashion sense. I used to think as long as the colors matched, it's whatever. Everything else was just too much to keep up with. I couldn't understand why people cared about this stuff.

And doing what I want? My mom put her foot down when she needed to. I thought it was unreasonable beyond words. In retrospect, she's always done her best as a mom.

I always felt that I was falling just a bit short, in regard to almost everything. So therefore, even happiness was just out of reach. It was always looming in front of me, taunting me, teasing me. All the things I wanted but couldn't have. I could see them in the distance. But my feet were planted firmly in place, refusing to move.

Low and behold, I finally realized that this mindset would keep happiness just out of reach forever if I allowed it to continue.

It was more than just a day late or dollar short or second place or runner up.

It was basically focusing on failure instead of success.

Improper focus on all the, "I could have, if only I would have, maybe I should have…" I now see that all of that is garbage. It's disgusting "thought-sludge" that holds you back from all that life has to offer.

There is no happiness when you look around at all of that… crap.

It makes up just a few layers. A few that you can peel off, dig up, whatever you need to do, to unleash what is beyond.

Happiness really is a conscious choice. It's a choice to get rid of all the false perceptions, expectations, assumptions, and lame BS that you tell yourself, and what you let the world tell you.

For years I allowed myself to play the victim in a story…

A sad tale where the protagonist always felt a page behind the storyline… where the light wasn't shining bright enough… where the words just didn't rhyme when they were supposed to.

Now I look at life with a tear in my eye, a smile on my face, and a giggle, and a sigh.

There's the rhyme that was always "supposed" to be.

I'm on the right page. I always have been. More than likely, you are too.

Perhaps the words were blurred. Or my vision on life wasn't where it needed to be yet. Or the lighting was too dim. Now the light allows itself to shine and the words find their way to rhyme.

Yes, as a child, I thought it was about having everyone like me, but now I see that it's about liking and loving yourself, and having certain people love and appreciate you for you, for everything you are and even what you are not.

I thought it was about being good at everything, now I see it's about being good at a few things that fuel your heart, mind, and soul… and putting your wholehearted efforts into what ignites your fires and focusing and dedicating to becoming a professional at your craft.

I thought it was about all A's. Accepting nothing less than perfection. Now I believe that we are meant to excel at some things and need to accept it is unhealthy to strive for perfection. Greatness, sure. But not perfection. We are each meant for something different. And that's a blessing.

I thought it was about being pretty. I later learned that feeling beautiful is what matters. Being a good person, being YOU, taking care of yourself, that is what makes you feel beautiful. The really pretty girls don't have it all just because they are pretty.

I thought it was about wearing nice clothes. Now, after years of watching the trends change, I laugh about it. Now, in my mind, "nice" clothes are whatever makes me feel good. It's not about the brand, or trend, or what people think. It's what about suits my personality or even my mood, at the time.

And...I thought happiness was about getting to do what I want, making my own choices. As a child of course, it was an unrealistic expectation. Doing what you want as a child has its limits.

But now as an adult... I realize it honesty is about doing what you truly want.

Happiness is about getting to make choices. It's choosing to be happy.

It's choosing who and what we allow to have an effect on us. And it's choosing which moments we embrace. Which endeavors we focus on. Which beliefs we hold and which we disregard.

It's all about what we want to do. To accomplish. To enjoy. To impact. To be.

Be what you WANT to be.
Be HAPPY if that is what you WANT.

The World, the Universe, the You of the past will high five you for it! And honestly, I will too!

*"We must experience the valleys
in order to appreciate the peaks."*

The Rock Bottom Moments -

Did you ever just really want to run,
Like really run the hell away?
As fast as your feet would move,
Until you hit the end of the earth and fade away?

Have you felt discouraged to the point of no return,
Like no matter what you'd somehow crash and burn.

Sick and sad, and completely lost alone.
Even if moments before your light had shone.

The answers just outside your grasp,
The light hidden by a shade of doubt,
The words right there at the tip of your tongue
But you cannot decipher what they're about.

Take the deepest of breaths in those moments of pain,
Feel the depths of emotion, soak in the rain,

For we often hit rock bottom, before we soar,
We feel we are less, before we strive for more.

We are just human, we are allowed to feel.
It reminds us we're alive, reminds us we're real.

It's ok to pout and to let the tears fall,
It's ok to metaphorically hit a wall.

And even if in that moment you want to run,
If in that moment you jump the gun,

You succumb to sadness, you straight up cry.

You let it out. Don't question why.

We deserve the moments we step back and release.
It allows the moments of calm, the stillness and peace.

Then we breath in deep, we start the next moment anew.
It's a bittersweet journey, yet we push on through.

"Adversity doesn't mean that you should give up on your mission. It only stops you if you give it permission.

So learn the lessons as they're given to you, and it will make it all worth it as your dreams come true."

Fear is the friend that will never leave us alone.
The love-hate companion, that makes itself present.
Especially in the times we beg it to be unknown.
It creeps up on us, with a sneer and a smile.
Grabbing our hand it its own, clutching it tight,
As if it has known how the wind would blow all awhile.
It tries so drastically to write the story we tell,
And we must rise above it, move forward and beyond,
Until we can someday thank it and bid it farewell.
For we know we have power inside us, that is stronger than fear,
And we may search for years, through difficult storms,
But the moment that defines us is greater than the shed of every tear.

Becoming Unstoppable -

What would be the outcome of lying in your bed,
hiding from the world, the covers pulled over your
head?

How would the world ever see what you truly are?
How could you be illuminated from the light of any
star?

What would happen if you pulled those covers down?
Would the effect change things, be something
profound?

Then, just what if you pulled those covers down low,
And let your smile radiate, let your light just glow?

What if you then put one foot on the floor,
Would you feel a difference, the world begging you for
more?

Then the second foot, plant it firm and strong,
Oh wow, is this where you truly do belong?

Broaden your shoulders, and stand yourself upright,
Ready to thrive in life, and ready to ignite.

Then raise your arms up, ready to full-on soar,
Telling all the world, "I'm not scared, anymore!"

Climb atop of the bed, a mountain your very own,
Show that world just how much that you have grown.

This is your life, no one chooses it but you,
You are the very one to see the dreams all through.

What would be the outcome of just lying in your bed?
No, my friend, you're meant to be unstoppable instead!

A Toast -

Yesterday, you are a ghost,
which to whom I raise this glass for a toast.

Thank you for your silence,
For your ways of making me learn on my own terms.

Today, you are a presence,
which to whom I raise this glass for a toast.

Thank you for your obstacles,
For your ways of making me tear down the walls in my way.

Tomorrow, you are a spirit,
which to whom I raise this glass for a toast.

Thank you for your uncertainty,
For your ways of making me pave my own path
in my pursuit for happiness.

*"We can obtain much wisdom in little time,
given the right teachers."*

Coulda, Woulda, Shouldas Tell Stories That You Don't Know Whether to Believe -

I certainly don't have it all figured out.

I fall. I fail. I make stupid mistakes. And occasionally I get too emotional and my anxiety comes in to play its ridiculous games.

Nope, not all figured out.

And that is ok.

I always used to think it was a "problem." I thought my shortcomings and screw-ups made me unworthy of getting my words out into the world. My "coulda, woulda, shouldas" tell me stories that I don't know whether or not to believe.

There was that lame "day late, dollar short" bullsh*t mindset.

Looking back, I can now pinpoint many of the events and the unkind words and the less successful moments that brought me to self-sabotage.

I think so many of us do this.

We focus on what we could have done, under different circumstances would have done, or what we perhaps... just maybe... but not certainly... it depends... let me think about it more.... should have done.

But instead think... if we did "that" particular thing, would we be who we are? If the past was altered would you be that which you are at this moment in time? Regardless of how you feel about current and present YOU… if any other decision or experience had altered things… you would not be the one with the story to tell, the passion to pursue, the help to give, the lesson to teach, the difference to make, the lives to change, the legacy to leave…

Do you get what I'm saying here?

I think perfection is stupid, honestly. I'd never claim it. I will strive to be the best ME until the day I die, but I will never, in regard to anything, even consider "perfection" to be a realistic thing. Far too often, people strive for perfection, often without realizing it.

We, (myself included) have had moments where we focus on how we lacked, how we missed the mark, even if we came just inches away. Why do we beat ourselves up? We are human. And not only is that alright, that there is beautiful.

My mentors say things like "Perfectly Imperfect. And Perfect Sucks." And I resonate with that 100%.

Recently, I've been focusing on my successes. But I'll be real with you, there have been plenty of failures, too. And I say that with a smile because I've learned and grown a "sh*t ton" from them.

I have come to understand that focusing on our great moments and milestones is what helps us press on. Life is not meant to be perfect, it is meant to be an adventure.

Have you ever read a book where everything works out just as hoped… no adversity… no setbacks… no struggle?

Have you heard someone tell a story where everything started out great, continued great, ended great...

People don't often tell stories or write books like that. No one would listen. No one would relate. They probably wouldn't even care.

We're put on this planet for our own reason, in our own season.

We are ALL meant for something.

It's not necessarily meant to be easy. It's the human experience. It's our story. There will be less than stellar moments, and heartache, tears, and a lot of crap to sort through.

There will also be laughter, friendships, love, success, beauty, and a sense of true purpose.

You don't need to have it figured out, friends.

Ride the wave and trust your heart. You are the hero of your story.

The kaleidoscope doesn't pause these days.

It's confusing at times.

It's frightening at times.

It's beautiful at times.

It doesn't stop to allow us to take a breath,

Or to indulge in the moment,

To just be and to see.

But the way we view it...

The movement, the colors, synergy, design.

No two of us see it exactly the same.

Yet somehow, we can align.

The kaleidoscope isn't the only one who can change.

Its spin is beyond our control,

But we can shift our perspective.

We are capable of adapting and yet remaining beautiful.

See that sparkle in the kaleidoscope's spin?

That is what you focus on.

That is what is within.

Belief -

I believe in karma and I believe in fate,

Not a breath too soon but not a moment too late.

I believe in tomorrow and I believe in today,

With a dream and ambition you can't take away.

Pause in the moment. -

Let me just pause for a brief moment in time. Because that, I'll admit, is not something I do enough.

There is always a rush, a brand-new dream, an idea, an inspiration… or sometimes a necessity or a deadline, truth be told.

But there is always a "something" that is pushing me forward, with this sense of guilt if I divert my focus.

I believe in forward motion, more than many even know.

I was a girl that used to wallow in the past. The mistakes, the heartbreak, the wondering and the doubt.

Then I became someone who suddenly decided to turn the car around.

Destination tomorrow, and rarely look back.

Then I came to learn that the beauty of life, and the truth in living… is the experience of it all.

I look back rather often, but I smile through the tears.

I look forward very often, and I anticipate the years.

I look at the present moment, and I befriend my fears.

Because sometimes I was scared to look back, afraid it may bring me down from the wave I was happy to ride.

I was scared to look ahead, I was unsure of what might be found.

Now I get those butterflies when I take a good look at today. Nervous, excited, and real.

There are crazy ups and downs along the way, and there is something to embrace in that adventure. It's about appreciation, gratitude, the ability to laugh at yourself in the most genuine way.

I look at how far I've come overall, knowing I'm on an uphill climb, smiling through the tears, and taking the next step in stride. All while I glace back and think, wow that's a long way down… look at how far I've come. In the blink of an eye I see those times that I felt like a hopeless failure in a sense, I see all the moments and milestones of the climb, and remind myself that progress is a process, and that is uniquely beautiful. It's the creation of our own story.

I love seeing others enjoy the adventure and seeing those as they realize that it *IS* an adventure.

There is something to be said about picking up puzzle pieces scattered across the floor, and one by one assembling them into something beautiful.

But I digress.

It is great to pause.

To stop. To release. To reflect and look forward.

To pause in. the. moment.

Take a deep breath, as deep as you can…

And reset.

"There is a bright side to nearly every situation.

Seek for the light and it will illuminate for you."

Ghost or Gold -

It's funny, the things we've been through and seen.
It's funny, the way we ponder and dream.
It's strange how these moments just pass us by,
And strange that time and again, we ask why.

It's a wild crazy chase for reason and trust.
It's a battle of heart, of is it love, is it lust?
It's a true here and now trial, do I live for today,
Or spend these moments just paving the way?

How can we answer, how can we understand?
With a dream in our heart, with a goal in our hand?
We hope all we can, we wish, and we thrive,
Just to feel that we are truly alive.

Never live as a ghost, with remorse or regret.
Your life is full of promise you haven't yet met.
Reach for the stars, and reach for the sky,
Never let life's moments just pass you by.

Hold onto the hearts whom you love you the most,
Let go of the past, raise your glass for a toast,
To today and tomorrow and the beauty it may hold,
This is your life, you choose if it's platinum or gold.

Soaring -

Close your eyes,
Get a glimpse of what your life can be.
Relax your thoughts,
Open your mind and set yourself free.

There is a story unfolding,
The legacy of you,
A breath of the words
of your dreams coming true.

Just listen.
The answers are there.
Take a moment to pause.
Inhale the truth in the air.

Moments are priceless,
Be wise how you spend.
Each second is a blessing
Just as each lesson, a friend.

This time now is precious,
Just let it reveal,

All the things that you are,
And all that you feel.

Allow your heart to uncover,
Your truth and your voice,
To hide or be seen,
You are blessed with the choice.

Make that decision,
Then open your eyes,
And begin that climb
To soaring the skies…

*"Forward and Upward, one step at a time.
That is progress.
That is success."*

Forgiveness and the Power to Move Forward -

(Spring 2019)

Not long ago, I watched a training on forgiveness. I have learned a lot about forgiveness in the past year, the most important takeaway being that forgiveness isn't only about the other person, it's about you. It's about releasing the burden that lays heavy on your heart so you can move on.

I've done a lot of forgiving in the past 10 months since I've begun to realize the weight it placed on me to hold such grudges. Many of those grudges I didn't even realize existed. I thought I had moved on. But they still played a big part in my memories, my current mindset, and who I have become. I desperately needed to release that so I could grow… so that I could be ME.

Through some trainings, tools, a podcast/exercise and journaling, and even some sessions that helped me explore what ages and memories triggered pain, I learned to release. My first ever FB Live on my page was publicly forgiving those who have wronged me and apologizing to anyone I have hurt in the past. And I also thanked them.

That was a huge step for me, there are a few instances that really pop into my head when I would think of what actions of others have played a hurtful role in my life. These instances would often include pain, just at the thoughts alone, raging in like it happened just yesterday.

Some of these things happened years ago. Up to 33 years ago, honestly.

They have accrued. Forgiveness isn't just about saying "I forgive you." There is a mental and emotional tie that you need to break and a hole you need to mend. It means release. Let it go. Cut off the emotional tie that the person, event, action, or words have on your heart.

It's not always easy to do, especially dependent on the weight it carries and the significant impact it has made on your life.

Often times, it's little things. They certainly didn't seem little at the time, or even now, but in the overall scheme of things…

A big part is finding the lessons and value.

I've been able to finally look back and see the good in what has happened "to me."

Holding grudges for other people's negative actions/mistakes, etc, does us no good. It does not serve us or our purpose in any way, other than to find the good in the circumstance and release, freeing up your heart and mind for good.

When I typed freeing up your heart and mind for good, I typed quickly and rather than "good," it said "god." Another meaningful typo.

So I made a typing "mistake", which ended up leading to encouraging, uplifting realization. I believe in signs from the Universe, and I believe that this was one. I know this was God confirming it for me. This writing, my path, my vision and mindset.

A little "God-Wink" remind me that mistakes are ok. Show yourself some grace. This comes right before I was about to get to my main point of this journaling, which is rather mind blowing now.

As I listened to the training, I thought about how much I have forgiven lately and actually had a hard time thinking of who and what to focus on forgiving for this "assignment." Then my coach began to talk about forgiving ourselves.

That was the kicker. Woah.

There's a person I held a serious grudge against, and that person was myself.

I "should" on myself all the time.

THAT is playing a toll on my heart. And my time.

All the "what if's" are energy-sucking vampires.

Truthfully, if I had done things differently, I wouldn't be here at this exact moment typing this. I wouldn't be on this particular path. The path I now finally found and LOVE.

Would different actions on my part made things better or worse? There is no way of knowing that and therefore is a waste of time to stress and ponder.

Move forward.

Through life, we all make mistakes, we all do things we aren't proud of and make decisions that are less than stellar. Even the greatest humans are still human.

They are less than perfection and that is just part of existence.

Forgive yourself. Regret just holds you back even when you are pushing forward.

We are in a constant tug of war with our past. Let go of the rope and watch it fall. *Then, you are free to soar.*

Tearfully and Beautifully Mine -

You can talk and judge, but you don't know,

you don't know all the things,

these things that make me, ME.

The pain and tears the worries and fears,

that hinder this optimistic and loyal heart.

I could try to explain, but what would I gain?

Another opinion, a judgment that based on YOUR life,

not mine?

You'd say I'm doing just fine.

Yeah, there's a smile on my face, whether it's out of place.

I try and try, I give my all, I get up and strive even when I fall.

But even I'm deserving of some tears now and then,

and I'm deserving of an honest friend.

It's not about the past or future or anything in between,

It's about MY chapter, my lyrics, my scene.

I'll never let anyone else make me live with regrets,

I choose my own battles, I make my own bets.

I sing my own song, and I write my own story,

And every day's dawn is a new chance for glory.

"Face your obstacles and stay on track,
for when you are determined there is <u>no</u> turning back."

Farewell Past -

You can't regret that which has caused you to grow,
Helped you to see and allowed you to know.

You can't undo the words just as you can't undo the math.
You can't change a past that's paved a path.

That path has molded you and guided you well,
Despite bridges burned and tears that fell.

Even times of despair, when bruised and defeated,
They brought meaning and glory to the times we've
succeeded.

You can't look back and blame your past.
With a smile and a nod, bid farewell at last.

You can step forward, a bit at a time,
With your head held high and walk a straight line.

You can open your heart and open your mind,
You don't yet know what you just might find.

Your Reflection -

Look in the mirror.
Stand there, my friend.
Look straight ahead,
Do not turn, do not bend.

Make eye contact.
Eyes open wide.
Look past the glare,
Look deep inside.

What stares back at you?
What speaks your voice?
Does it tease and taunt?
Or goes it give you a choice?

Be real, and be honest,
What's the reflection you see?
Is it masked and uncertain,
Or does it beg to be free?

Does it have something to say?
Does it ask to thrive?
And does it look past today,
And promise to be alive?

Ask it, bet it, and challenge it, too.
Look beyond the reality,
 you thought that was you.
There is something deeper, unravel it now,
Pull back the layers and find you somehow.

It may not be easy, it may take some time,
But when your true colors show, your stars will align.

"If you do not consider failures to be failures, you will always find success."

The Letter "A" -

(This one is based on a friend's social media post that simply said "A". While that post was accidental, it received many comments and sparked something within its readers.)

Never underestimate the ripple you can make,
Sometimes just a letter is all that it will take.

If you don't put it out there, never will you know,
How strong the wave can be, and how far it can go.

You can provoke thoughts and emotions, and laughter on the way,
And the pebble that hits the water, can be just a single "A".

Others feel the effect of that ripple, from both far and near,
The "A words" start popping up, and you see the wave appear

It gains such momentum, with each soul who adds a word.
To think the post was by accident, the thought is so absurd.

Apparently, it was meant to be, and all the "A" words will inspire.
Sometimes you light a spark, other times you'll start a fire.

A ripple can begin easily, we see now that it's true,
Perhaps the greatest ripples, will start with "I" and "U."

"Waves are beautiful proof that the ripple effect is real."

Your Decision to Be -

There are moments in life, that you just need to BE.
Take a deep breath, say "World, I am ME."

There are times that some will just not understand,
They may not be ready to hold your hand.

It's those times that are most pivotal, so just truly be YOU.
Let truth take its course and your light shine anew.

We are meant to learn lessons, we must play life's game.
Or else we succumb to remaining the same.

Which is not what we are meant for, we live to thrive.
The purpose of life is being truly alive.

We aren't meant for perfection, we are meant to be real,
To experience, to grow, to learn and to feel.

No one is flawless, in a realistic view.
Have you ever read a story that's perfect all through?

That's just not the way, life has ups and downs.
Just hold your head high and know no bounds.

Never let the world stop you, from glistening in gold,
Be honest, be genuine, be fearless and bold.

That's easier said than done, this I do know.
But it's the grasp on the goal, that helps us to grow.

Life is so precious, and it will not last forever,
There is beauty we'll bask in and storms we must weather.

The beauty is in perspective, this moment is yours.
Will you drown in the sorrow, or will you swim to the shores?

Be You, Regardless -

There are people in the escapade,
the blissful, purposeful, masked charade,

That do not understand, no matter how we try,
They doubt us, pause us, and they question why.

Any do we stop, due to their insistent glare?
Of do we thrive and strive to get somewhere?

Their intentions may be good, they may be real,
But do they understand a damn about how we feel?

Odds are they do not, and it makes a mark,
And sometimes it can even dull our spark.

But my friend, please know that you have a choice,
Your determination can speak louder, it's *your voice.*

If you insist on being heard, it's louder than the doubt,
Louder than the fears and all the past has been about.

*"When we close our eyes, we soar the skies.
When we open them wide, we are awake for the ride."*

Dream to Vision -

A dream is a vision that our heart creates,
It's the tomorrow that patiently awaits.

It is our yearning, our vow, to reach our star,
The sight we imagine, if we stare afar.

What we know we can do, if we just zero in.
It's the challenge we tackle, the reward if we win.

It is our innermost soul, the gleam in our eyes,
As we stand tall and courageous, look up to the skies.

A dream is more than a wish, more than a hope or desire,
It's the flint of the match that fuels the fire.

Some may say something is only a dream,
But do they understand the sparkle, the strength of the gleam?

It's bright and it's beautiful and emits a true glow.
Stronger than thoughts or what you think you may know.

A real dream is powerful, it's the epitome of real.
It's everything within, that a person can feel.

And why do we have them? Because we are born for it,
Before the rest of life's crap makes us mourn for it.

Our time is limited, the dreams tell us to thrive,
To live out the vision, to be fully alive.

Dreams are the question, the answer as well.
The purpose we serve, the story we tell.

Yes, a dream is a vision the soul will create,
You've been created to chase it before it's too late.

*"Wake up each day with a smile on your face
and The Universe will smile back."*

Self-Discovery -

Not long ago I felt grounded, with no certain reason why.
Now I want to feel the wind beneath me, as I spread my wings to fly.

I felt a little bit broken, like I was missing a vital piece.
Now I will inhale all my truth, and the doubt I will release.

Occasionally I felt worthless, like I didn't have what it will take.
Now I will love me for me, and the pivotal moves I'll make.

Sometimes I felt unqualified, like the knowledge wasn't mine,
Now I realize I have it in me, I've had it all this time.

I guess I was just a little scared, what would others say?
Now I understand this life is mine, I'll live it my own way.

I was uncertain of my purpose, what am I meant to be?
Now a voice inside me speaks so loudly and tells me to be Me.

All these limiting thoughts, they are part of life, it's true.
But what if we leave them behind, a start this future off anew?

If we leave everything that held us back, bid it thank you and farewell,
Close the door on that book, there's a brand-new story to tell.

What can we create, and write, and draw and proudly say?
What can evolve from believing, in a beautiful new day?

Not long ago I was lost, but myself I have finally found,
And unveiling that realization, is truly a life-altering sound.

"Inspiration is the starting point.

It creates the dream,

which develops into the vision,

which transforms into your reality."

What You Are -

There's a bit beyond believing the things that we can see.

A breath beyond believing in the things that we can be.

A step beyond the know-how, the things now in our hold,

A step beyond the moment, a blissful gleam of gold.

What if you are that person who is meant for so much more?

What if you are that power that can open a sealed door?

What if you are the lyric that is added to the song,

Or the paining of the picture, what if this is where you do belong?

What if you are the answer to what others strive to know,

The light that ignites and sets off a stunning glow?

What if there is no if, what is there is only what is real,

What if you are everything that your mind and heart do feel?

What if there are no limitations, if you are everything you're meant?

What if all the past pain and failure are time so very well spent?

Maybe there is reason, maybe there is rhyme,

Maybe we didn't realize that we knew it all this time.

We are all meant for something, that is greater than just a dream,

Success and truth and purpose, a life that has a theme.

Tomorrow is not promised, we only make a promise to our own,

To show the world we have learned, we've thrived, and we have grown.

It's all about the moment, the message and the lesson, too.

The light in utter darkness, the voice that speaks so true.

Your Word of the Year -

What if you just COMMIT to SIMPLIFY to a single thing?
To FOCUS on one GOAL. What JOY could that bring?

Do you want to INSPIRE the world,
to RADIATE a POSITIVE vibe?
To ORGANIZE real CHANGE,
or CREATE an AUTHENTIC tribe?

Maybe you ASPIRE to SPARKLE brighter,
to ILLUMINATE and SHINE,
To move FORWARD with TRUST and FAITH,
to see the stars ALIGN.

Or UNLEASH your true POTENTIAL,
EXPLORE some UNCOMMON ground,
ENJOY the CALM of SILENCE in your mind,
an EXTRAORDINARY sound.

Perhaps it's a year of RECONCILIATION,
or HEALING just as well,
DETERMINATION to find some BALANCE
or WRITE the story you will tell.

Or of FAMILY and VALUES,
PRIORITIZING what matters most of all,
Having a MISSION placed on your HEART
and answering the call.

As we SEEK for FRIENDSHIPS,
with whom we COINCIDE,
To UPLIFT each other and SOAR together
on this EPIC ride.

We may need to TIDY up our space,
DISCOVER our WORTH and FLOW,
Show PERSISTANCE to IGNITE,
so we can RADIATE and GLOW.

Be BOLD & FEARLESS when we're tested,
be PRESENT in the MOMENTS as they are.
Find a sense of PEACE, HEALTH and WEALTH,
as we chase the brightest star.

STRIVE for overall WELLNESS,
hold the SPACE that's all our own.
CHERISH the OPPORTUNITY
and VENTURE into the UNKNOWN.

We have the FREEDOM to DECIDE
just what we DESERVE.
So we may FULFILL our DESTINY,
and HELP those we're meant to SERVE.

It takes real STRENGTH to PERSEVERE,
sometimes we must show GRACE,
Be CONFIDENT and INTENTIONAL
and have a SMILE on your face.

Be BRAVE to CONQUER all those doubts,
RELEASE and then BECOME,
We must LEARN from our JOURNEY,
no matter where we're from.

We may need to display RESILIANCE,
or FINISH what we START,
Take ACTION towards our DREAMS,
ENCOURAGE others to PLAY their part.

IMAGINE taking the time to BREATHE,
to APPRECIATE the moment,
Be MINDFUL of your PURPOSE,
hold it, seize it, OWN it.

There is BEAUTY and TRUTH in everything,
if we just PAUSE and SEE.
At times we need to DO,
at times we just need to BE.

EXPAND our minds and OVERCOME,
RESPECT and just BELIEVE.
IMPLEMENT the LESSONS,
there's so much to ACHIEVE.

It's an ADVENTURE full of ABUNDANCE,
show GRATITUDE and LOVE,
With a forward-motion MINDSET,
we can RISE above.

We may need to STOP and LISTEN
before we PLAN and BEGIN,
And there is POWER in CONSISTENCY,
in a CHALLENGE we can win.

EMBRACE all that is placed in your world,
REFLECT and UNDERSTAND,
There is a CAUSE for each endeavor,
yet the EFFECT can be so GRAND.

If you just remain OPEN and WILLING
to TRANSCEND and TRANSFORM,
You can DESIGN your LEGACY
and WITHSTAND any storm.

FORGIVENESS can be the key,
just as much as LAUGHTER,
And the YES or NO of today,
may lead to your HAPPY ever after.

A word creates a VISION,
lets us CELEBRATE who we are.
GROWTH takes real ENDURANCE,
more than a WISH upon a star.

If hindsight is 20/20,
you can be the one to STAND and say,
"This will be the year I have my BREAKTHROUGH
and I find my way...

The year I grasped the OPPORTUNITY
to CHOOSE a word and THRIVE,
The year I chose to LIVE in the NOW
and truly feel ALIVE!"

"If you want to be truly unstoppable, create a legacy.

Then not even death can stop you."

Passing of Time -

Many years and many tears,
Lie as memories in my past.
Continued belief, shelter from grief,
Will help my world unfold at last.

I stare at the days, the ways,
That my yesterdays fade to the night,
And dream of the beautiful tomorrow
When darkness turns into light.

"At times we must allow others the space to grow, even if it means somewhat letting go."

Vulnerability, Changes and Answers-

You know that your perspective is improving when you don't always need to search for the good in things, because the good often jumps out at you.

For years I took pride in my optimistic perspective. My husband had teased me by giving me the nickname, "Optimist Prime."

I had a way of pulling out the good and seeing the best, usually through writing. Yet, that optimism wavered at times

I began to let it slip, and it was replaced by less stellar feelings. No longer was I the happy and upbeat self that I had grown up as.

The years and tears had taken a toll on me.

I didn't realize I was lost... until it was time to find myself again.

All the doors around me opening and closing... it was exhausting. I didn't know which ones to step through, my hesitation left me feeling the breeze in my face as doors slammed shut before me. The winds of adversity blew dust in my face, blurring the reality, and I could feel the sting. I felt powerless. Where was that strength, that determination? Did I drop it along the way?

The road behind me was filled with memories. Amazing times and heartbreak. The emotions used to fluctuate, within seconds, and they controlled me rather than I them.

So, I left them on that road. Some are dust and dirt. Others are a beautiful flower on the side of the road, or a sparkling pond with its occasional ripple creating a beautiful effect.

Not everything is beautiful, but so many things can be.

Not everything has good to it, yet so much can.

It's fun to not have to dig for the "bright side", to over-analyze, to make excuses.

It's freeing.

I had a serious attachment to my old home and my old life. It was purely based on comfort zone. I realize that now, but I didn't then.

I was torn between feeling it was holding me back and desperate to propel forward and being terrified to take steps and to leave the past behind, where the past belongs.

I thought that leaving my surroundings behind, dismissing certain people in life and stopping them from shaking my perspective and confidence, and tearing down the barriers that had amounted and kept me from being me would be a difficult task.

It was.

But in all honesty, it was easier than I had anticipated, because I knew deep down it was right.

We all have a place.

The place for me, right here and right now, is to be sitting at my desk in my office writing, while I hear my children's laughter in the other room as they play.

I'm not meant to be "spinning in circles" like I was. My mind full of ideas, wishes, dreams, goals... and excuses, reasons, doubts, uncertainties.

I'm meant for so much more.

It doesn't really matter how many people see it, but I know there are many who do.

I see it. I know it. I feel it.

I was lost. It was hard. It was confusing and sad.

But now, I have found me. I have found my purpose.

My joy. My ambitions. My worth.

If you are lost, the greatest thing you can do is look into your heart and soul. There you will find the change, the turning point, the "shift," if you will.

There you will find truth.

There you will find yourself.

Pause.
Indulge in the silence.
Breathe.
See.
Trust.
This moment is golden.
This moment is yours.
The stillness reflects the beauty,
Of life, of love, of truth...
Design this moment.
It is up to you.
Moments are what you make of them.
Just pause.
And Create.

Acceptance & Growth -

There are times in life you may be misunderstood,
Just look deep within you'll see all the good.

It's not always about what the rest of them see,
Understand that and you'll set yourself free.

Each person is different, their eyes do not see the same,
We've been dealt different hands, there should be no
blame.

If we meet a million people in the course of our time,
No two will every have the same exact story, same rhyme.

That's a bit intimidating, but gorgeous the same,
We each hold our own dice, we play our own game.

There are rules we must follow and some we'll make on
our own,
Based on our strategies and how much we have grown.

But we can learn to love, even when opinions collide,
It's not about what we think, it's about what's inside.

The values and love, the true overall,
The extending the help, to lift up those who fall.

They could offer me a new hand, or a new roll of the dice,
But I'd choose this again and again, and never think twice.

From One Inspired Dreamer to Another -

It's imperative to Dream Big, yet you must chase the dreams. It's ok to pause in the moments as you celebrate the milestones. But then you must continue, set your sights on the goals but enjoy and appreciate the journey. Sometimes you will fall or fail. You are human. That's not a fault, it's a blessing. You learn from the pain and even from the bullsh*t. You are growing daily. Sometimes tears are a part of that growth. Let 'em flow. Enjoy the release. You'll feel stronger afterwards. Whoever said that strong people never cry are lying. Smile at yourself in the mirror. You are the only person in the world that sees that exact reflection. You are unique, inside and out. That's pretty damn cool when you think about it. Laugh often. Laughter is the best medicine one could ever self-prescribe. It turns a frown upside down in an instant. Breathe deeply out in fresh air. Notice beauty. Plant your feet firmly on the ground. Plant seeds in the ground too. Watch the growth, you are the same. Water the plants and water your soul. There is no changing yesterday. You can often adjust the way you perceive the outcome by changing your perspective. Recognize if your perspective sucks. Sometimes it may. Sometimes you'll speak before you think and sometimes you'll be sorry. Say it. Fess up. Be real and raw. We are gifted a limited amount of time on this planet. Don't spend it regretting, wondering why.

Accept it, be inspired. Fluff your feathers and fly. We aren't able to change the world alone, but we can be the spark and the pebble that affects the rest. We can be more, see more, do more and achieve more, just by being real and determined to grasp the dreams. There is adversity. It's not going anywhere. Learn to stand up straight and look it in the eye. Smile, even if it's with your eyes. Smiles are an energy beyond measure. If you're overwhelmed, create a not-to-do list. Scribble down some things you don't need to worry about. Immediate gratitude, and the things you must do will be less of a burden. See the love. Notice the good. Believe in the future, and smile at the past. Even if the road is broken and shattered. You.... are not. You can't change others but you can shift yourself. Other people's opinions don't really matter. That's their prerogative. Just like you can think what you want. So think good things. Look for light in the darkness. Extend an olive branch. Get actual sleep. Dream good dreams, whether sleeping or awake. You choose your conscious dreams, remember that. You decide your own thoughts. That's important. Let your loved ones know they are loved. Let yourself know you are loved. And, of course, never let the world stop you from shining brightly. This, this is when the world needs that glimmer and shine most of all. Trust, immerse, glisten and be.

No Matter What You Do, You're a Writer

Many people say that they are not a writer. I beg to differ.

We are all writers on a daily basis… *we write our life story*

Your life is your creation. No one else is in charge of your story but you.

You choose the genre; will your life be a thriller, a romance, humorous? Maybe your story shines in the travel section, or self-help. Or perhaps it's actually a well-rounded assortment of genres (like mine!)

Then there is your plot… what happens in your story. Some people outline this (to-do lists, goals, dream boards!) and some just wing-it. What happens each day? Is it routine or is each day a new venture? It's completely up to you. YOU'RE the writer!

You choose your supporting characters and how they influence you, the main character. Do these characters lift you up or bring you down? Do they truly "support"? Will they play a significant role in your story?

It is up to you to determine when one chapter concludes, and another begins. This is one of the greatest privileges of being the writer. The ability to shift direction. To close and open doors. To choose how and when to progress.

Most importantly, you develop the main character, **You**! Will that character be the protagonist? Or more like an antagonist in their own story? Do they stand tall when faced with adversity? Or do they crouch in the shadows, fearfully hiding from their own adventure? Do they smile often, do they laugh? Do they cry to release their feelings when their story gets overwhelming? You develop that character every single day. Your words and actions are continuously writing the description of who that main character IS. You can make him/her amazing and memorable, if you choose.

Will your story be timeless? Will it be appreciated by many? When you write the final chapter, will it be everything you wanted it to be?

You have it in you to do so.

So dear "writer", pick up your pen and write. And keep on writing, until your ink runs out...

*Strive to make your "I AM"
greater than your "I WAS"*

*Every.
Single.
Day.*

My Story -

"Many years ago, an 8-year-old rhymed about a mother hen,
One that never gave up, despite not knowing how or when.

Smiling at her parents, "I'm going to be an author!" she said.
And she'd hide under her covers, reading & writing in her bed.

Filling up notebooks with poetry and stories over the years,
Some scribbles of hope, and some stained with tears.

Life written out daily in rhyme and in verse,
A little notebook, in case, kept in her purse.

This intensified in her teens, during such a trivial stage.
Every emotion and experience found its words upon a page.

The love to write continued with stories, books, and quotes,
Hundreds of ideas jotted down on pink post-it notes.

It continued through her 20s and 30s just the same.
She needed inspiration to take action and suddenly it came.

She thought back on her past, of that 8-year-old little girl,
The one who had two big dreams in the whole wide world.

To be a mother and a writer, the goals were set in stone.
She was meant for both, in her heart she'd always known.

At 35, she was a mom of four, so that dream had come true.
Which now left the writing, so she knew what she had to do.

Smiling at her family, "I'm going to be an author!" again she said.
And took all the thoughts & words that were living in her head.

It's time to make them come alive, the dreams & words as well,
And get back up after falling (and trust me, oh she fell!)

Persistence and patience, the latter was rather hard.
Some of the battles left her ego bruised and scarred.

But that's the thing with dreaming, if you want it to come true,
You push on and stop at nothing, it's just what you must do.

That little girl is still there, hidden under her grown disguise,
And now and then she sees the world through a child's eyes.

Life had taken a winding route, the vision blurred for a while,
But now there's passion and purpose, with every child's smile.

So tell that 8-year-old self, and tell that Mother Hen,
If you ever do stop dreaming, then just start again… "

When the voice in your head says, "You Can't,"

just smile and whisper, "Watch Me!"

IN CONCLUSION...

I waited until the "last minute" to write this, which was intentional. I'm not usually a last- minute kind of person, so I had to honestly force myself to wait.

I wanted to be at the point where this book is so close to being in your hands (or on your screen) to write these words.

If you resonated with something, anything in this book, I am forever grateful.

I hope you enjoyed it, that it inspired you in some way, encouraged you to chase your goals and dreams and helped you realize you aren't alone in this world.

Please know that despite how open and vulnerable I am in this book, it was still a leap out of my comfort zone to compile all of this together.

Though I have done it before with "Hey World, I'm Someone Too!" I was younger when I wrote that.

This book displays the lessons and emotions of someone who knows a little bit more about the world, whose dreams reach higher and farther than before.

I've shared a lot of this with the world, in bits and pieces over the years.

Now, here it is all together, almost an autobiography, that tells a collective tale of how beautifully broken we can be and reassemble in a way that is even greater than we ever were before.

I want you to realize that every moment is a new opportunity to smile, see the beauty, resonate with others, leave a footprint, teach a lesson, learn one, laugh, dance, dream, cry it out or find yourself again.

Life, its adventure, and the journey of growth and change is an ongoing process.

I've gone through a lot, but I believe wholeheartedly that the great achievements in life are worth the struggle, effort, and strength we must achieve from within.

Our past creates us, our present strengthens us and creates the memories we'll treasure, and the future… well, that is the unwritten story, and we hold the pen.

There may be hints and teasers. Perhaps many predictions and hopes. That is the next chapter in the series, the story, the legacy that YOU are creating.

I'm proud to feel unleashed, but my goal now, is that you feel unleashed as well.

Have you been what has held you back? Your internal thoughts, your worries and self-doubt, your but what if's, or I cant's…?

I've been there. I understand, and I believe with all of my heart that the world needs YOU TO UNLEASH!

You have it within you. If you are reading this, this is my nudge to you.

So take the time, gather the courage, and find your spark so that you may live up to your greatest and fullest potential.

Make this life precious and memorable, full of impact, beauty, and love.

It's time to <u>unleash</u>!

The possibilities are endless.

There is a grand adventure that awaits each and every inspired dreamer.

If you'd like to go on the journey together…

*Join the unleashed adventure and visit
cassandralennox.com*

Subscribe for a free downloadable poem that you can print and hang up as a reminder of the beautiful life you are meant for.

This will also give you access to the Chain of Inspiration newsletter, with new monthly quotes, poems, journals and offers.

The Inspiration Chain is a reminder that we have the ability to create an incredible ripple effect, one link at a time, through encouragement, support, friendship, understanding and a willingness to be a light in the world.

Live the life you were meant for, my friends.

That ripple creates the wave.

Like the storm, the stars, and the sunlight, we have the power deep within.

Let's unleash it!

Made in the USA
Coppell, TX
22 February 2021